MAKING SENSE OF BEHAVIOUR

CHALLENGING CONFRONTATION:

Information and Techniques

for School Staff

by

Rob Long

A NASEN PUBLICATION

Published in 1999

© Rob Long

All rights reserved. No part of this publication may be reproduced or transmitted in any form or by any means, electronic, mechanical, photocopying, recording, or otherwise without the prior permission of the publishers.

ISBN 1 901485 11 0

The right of Rob Long to be identified as author of this work has been asserted by him in accordance with the Copyright, Designs and Patents Act 1988.

Published by NASEN.
NASEN is a company limited by guarantee, registered in England and Wales. Company No. 2674379.
NASEN is a registered charity. Charity No. 1007023.

Further copies of this book and details of NASEN's many other publications may be obtained from the Publications Department at its registered office: NASEN House, 4/5 Amber Business Village, Amber Close, Amington, Tamworth, Staffs. B77 4RP.
Tel: 01827 311500; Fax: 01827 313005
Email: welcome@nasen.org.uk; Website: www.nasen.org.uk

Cover design by Raphael Creative Design.
Typeset in Times by J. C. Typesetting and printed in the United Kingdom by Stowes (Stoke-on-Trent).

Contents

Preface	4
Introduction	5
Confrontations and personal stress	6
Controlling our behaviour	11
Confrontation Inhibitors	16

Preface

CHALLENGING CONFRONTATION: Information and Techniques for School Staff is one of eight booklets in the series *Making Sense of Behaviour* by Rob Long. The others are *Exercising Self-control; Developing Self-esteem through Positive Entrapment for Pupils facing Emotional and Behavioural Difficulties; Friendships; Understanding and Supporting Depressed Children and Young People; Not Me, Miss! The Truth about Children who Lie; Supporting Pupils with Emotional and Behavioural Difficulties through Consistency;* and *Learning to Wave: Some Everyday Guidelines for Stress Management.*

Challenging Confrontation gives information and techniques for teachers to use when dealing with argumentative, angry and difficult pupils. *Supporting Pupils with Emotional and Behavioural Difficulties through Consistency* advocates a whole-school approach for low-level misbehaviours whilst *Learning to Wave* is written for teachers themselves. It contains advice about coping with the stress which might arise from dealing with children with behavioural problems.

The other five titles give practical ideas and information for teachers to use with children with worrying behaviours in their classes. These are written to help teachers both understand and change some of the difficulties that children might experience (depression, lack of self-control, low self-esteem, friendship problems and lying).

Each book stands alone but when read as a set the behavioural issues and their solutions overlap and this emphasises the need for positive and consistent strategies to be put into place throughout the school.

Acknowledgements
The author and publishers wish to express their grateful thanks to Lorna Johnston, Agnes Donnelly and Dorothy Smith for their helpful suggestions and comments.

Challenging Confrontation:
Information and Techniques for School Staff

Introduction

Few of us receive any instruction or guidance about managing confrontations yet in our schools and classrooms confrontation is now a fact of life. While many school staff cope very effectively, there are a large number of us who find it distressing and exhausting. The more we can understand confrontation the more effectively we can manage it. There are two common mistakes we make when dealing with argumentative, angry and difficult pupils.

1. We allow ourselves to become trapped by our own anger.
2. We become trapped in a cycle of escalating confrontation.

We are all aware of children who wear our patience down through repetitive acts of disruption, often petty, as well as those who openly challenge adult authority. There are also those who are emotionally volatile and explode with rage at apparently trivial frustrations.

This booklet will:

- provide skills to defuse confrontations
- enable staff to feel more in control
- provide a model for win-win outcomes
- safeguard our own emotional welfare

This booklet will not deal with physical restraint. The confrontations dealt with here are those that most of us, most of the time, manage well. But there are times when we are less than happy with the way we responded. We may even feel that we made the situation worse.

Some examples would include:

- The pupil who never seems to stop until you've lost your temper.
- The pupil who calmly challenges your authority.
- The pupil who uses obscene language to vent their anger.

How can school staff avoid taking such behaviours personally? It is easy to say, "You shouldn't let it get to you." But how do you stop it?

It is easy to think after the event of what you wanted to say or do, but how do you keep calm when you're in the middle of it?

There are no simple "quick fix solutions". Remember that while there are simple solutions to every complex problem - they are usually wrong.

Part of the difficulty with confrontations is that we think they don't happen often enough to justify us making time to learn the necessary skills. We believe that "Positive Behaviour Management" approaches will work with all our troubled and troublesome pupils. But sadly the pupils have not read the same book or attended the same course as we have. Pupils who have developed confrontation strategies over a number of years, as ways of coping in school, are not likely to change immediately.

We need to understand the process and mechanics of confrontation to enable us to manage situations positively. If we don't, then we will be swept along and at times do things that will actually make matters worse.

The power of conflict to attract attention
Conflict is naturally interesting to us because it can threaten our survival. As a result we are programmed to attend to it, it demands our attention. The media people know this and use it to catch people's interest. The next time you watch a soap on television, count just how often any "mini scene" has conflict in it. There are people shouting excessively or using threatening behaviour. Conflict is being used to manipulate our interest. It is only when we are aware of this that we can make an informed choice as to whether we wish to be so manipulated.

Confrontations and personal stress

There are three questions that need to be answered:

- Why do we react aggressively to confrontations which are of limited threat?
- Why do we overreact with some children and under-react with others?
- Why do we become frightened and passive in conflict situations?

The answers lie in this diagram.

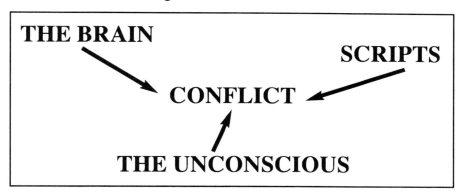

1. The brain

The brain can be divided into three parts, the reptile brain, the mammalian brain and the thinking brain. The reptile brain controls basic functions, breathing, eating etc. It is the mammalian brain that controls our emotions. It is also here that long-term memories are stored which explains why childhood memories are often strongly linked with emotions. The thinking brain is the one we are consciously aware of as we use it to plan our lives and solve problems.

To help us survive we evolved quick reactions to signs of threat. These "triggers" in the environment cause specific emotions that make us react in set ways. Our nervous system is the same as that of our ancestors who lived in the jungle. There are certain cues that trigger the mammalian brain into action with strong emotional arousal; the flight or fight response. If the mammalian brain believes it is under threat then it quickly sends out messages to protect us. But because it is not directly in touch with the world it can cause us to respond in less than appropriate ways. In a confrontational situation we are having our "alarm button" pressed. Instead of doing what we do under normal situations, namely

FEEL   **THINK**   **ACT**

the high level of arousal causes us to go from

FEELING straight to ACTION.

At the initial stages of confrontation emotional arousal is energising. We are ready for action. We are sharper in processing and responding to information. But if we continue to become more and more aroused, we are overwhelmed and lose the ability to think rationally. At this stage we may experience a "freeze reaction" or panic causing our behaviour to become erratic and unpredictable. At this stage we are at the top of the "anger mountain" (see below.) This model applies equally to adults and children. If we allow ourselves to be pushed to the top of our arousal curve then we will react "*as if*" we are in a completely unmanageable situation and our only hope is an extreme reaction. Panic or excessively aggressive behaviour can now be seen as "normal behaviour in abnormal circumstances".

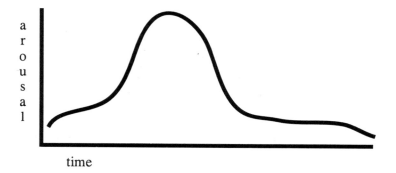

The Anger Mountain

This is how we can get drawn into the confrontational spiral. We raise our voice in response to being shouted at. Our arms become offensive weapons as we point with our index finger. We stand square-on to look bigger. We maintain hostile eye contact. We are reflecting the hostile messages we are receiving. Because these are largely unlearned patterns we will react in the same way to an angry adolescent or a young child. However, with the young child, we are more able to block our reactions because we are also receiving messages that elicit care and support on account of the child's facial features, size and tone of voice. It can be easier to control our emotions with some pupils than with others. This is not to say that there will not be times when even the young child will trigger negative responses.

2. The role of scripts

How we respond to confrontations can be plotted on a continuum. While we can move along it we can each see how we typically respond in conflict situations.

PASSIVE **ASSERTIVE** **AGGRESSIVE**

Clearly some of us have a calmer disposition than others. We each have a different temperament and some of us are naturally more relaxed than others. Each of us is biologically unique, except identical twins, and we have each been socialised uniquely by our family. In our families we were influenced as to how to behave and how to think. We learned which emotions were acceptable to show in public and which were not.

As a result as an adult we may not feel happy about showing certain emotions. As a culture most of us are not very good at either expressing anger or dealing with confrontations. Equally there are many who find it difficult to express affection, or feel tears are a sign of weakness and should not be shown. (This is still true for many males - hence the stiff upper lip.)

We each carry with us "scripts" which set how we are to think, feel and act and are reflected in the ways in which we approach the world. They are neither completely good nor bad. They are a mixture, with advantages as well as disadvantages. For example, many people carry a "please others" script. This has many positive attributes, but taken too far causes as many problems as it solves. For us the script that is most relevant is, "be strong". This one will put pressure on us to manage situations of conflict under the internal threat that to fail or run away is a sign of weakness. In conflict situations those of us with this internal script will move towards the aggressive end of the continuum when dealing with conflicts. The internal messages will be "How dare they behave like that, I'll show them who is boss."

Alternatively people who carry a "can't cope" script will become passive and withdraw from the conflict. They may feel a tendency to freeze in the face of aggression. Their internal message now will be "I'm frightened, I can't cope with this."

The more we are aware of the scripts we carry the more we can decide how helpful they are. Remember they are ways of coping we learned as children in our families. We might ask, "Do I always have to be strong?" "Must I always avoid anger?"

I am not saying that our scripts are wrong, but I am saying there are times when they may be unhelpful.

3. The unconscious

The final piece of our jigsaw is our own unconscious. This carries emotional memories from way back. It carries pleasant and unpleasant memories. We know that such emotional memories exist through our everyday experiences. Have you ever had a sudden flashback to a childhood emotional memory that was triggered by a smell or a taste? You could not have searched for the memory because it became part of you before you could talk. Well, some children and people can similarly trigger off emotions in us. The unconscious is not rational, it is not directly in touch with the outside world. Have you ever wondered why one 7 year-old can touch your caring side to the point that you could take them home and adopt them? They are "likeable rogues" despite their verbally aggressive behaviour. While on the other hand you genuinely believe that another 7 year-old has been sent to punish you, they seem "evil" and determined to refuse every effort you make to help them. Both children are 7 years old and they both behave in a not dissimilar manner. But our emotional responses are very different.

So what can we do?

You may feel that this information makes you feel even more helpless. But remember we have the Thinking Brain.

- If we are aware of the triggers that can lead to aggressive behaviours - we can learn to use those that inhibit or block aggression.
- If we are aware of the scripts we carry that are not helping us - we can challenge them and develop new ones.
- If we feel we are being influenced negatively by a strong "dislike" with no rational reasons - then we can take action to build a better relationship and reduce the unconsciousness's influence. (I think Freud's dream was to let the conscious, informed mind curb the impulses of the unconscious uninformed mind, a bit like education really!)

Controlling our behaviour

Signs and triggers
There are times when we can tell that a child is "wound up". Their behaviour tells us this. It is sometimes described as the "head in the hood" syndrome. As soon as you see them you know that they are tense and you modify your behaviour accordingly. The worst event is when such cues are ignored or misread and the adult carries on cajoling a child. It is as bad as looking for a gas leak with a match.

Warning signs
- agitated and fidgety
- facial colour deepens then goes pale
- breathe faster
- perspire
- have dilated pupils
- speak louder and faster
- move more quickly
- have tense muscles, contorted face
- hunched shoulders
- easily distractible/not focused

Remember from the child's viewpoint their body is being triggered into an "emergency response reaction". They are being prepared for flight or fight.

What to do
Non-verbal communication
When a child is angry and/or confrontational their behaviour, not them, will be trying to push our "button" and cause us to behave equally aggressively. (Have you ever noticed how we mirror each other's behaviours?) At such times we need to check our own behaviour to avoid being drawn into "knee jerk" reactions.

AVOID
Squaring up:
> Face-to-face positions are challenging so introduce an angle. If you imagine facing the person with both feet pointing ahead, shift your balance on to one foot. This will automatically make you swing the other out and move the upper half of your body around and away from the confrontational position.

Invading personal space:
> We all have an area around us of personal space. It is usually around 6-8 inches (18 cms). To enter it is to be invasive, so aim to stay just outside. If you are too far away then you can seem aloof, evasive and possibly uncaring. But it is worth remembering that habitually aggressive individuals tend to have larger personal space, so err on the side of caution.

Mood mirroring:
> When we relate with each other we tend to mirror each other's body positions. We also reflect their emotional tone. If you are talking to someone who is down, you will bring your mood down to reflect theirs. When working with a child who is angry we can too easily fuel their mood through becoming equally angry.

Threatening movements:
> Waving arms around, folding them, pointing with the index finger are all threatening movements and will fuel the confrontation. Try to hold them or keep them behind your back. The best gestures are ones where you show your palms or where you use them to support your message, both hands used slowly pushing downwards with the palms down and saying "Let's calm down."

DO

Match their mood:
> Remaining incredibly calm when someone is extremely agitated does not help matters, so don't remain calm - but reflect an increase in emotional level towards sorting matters out. "I can see that you are upset, and I am really, really concerned about how this is affecting your behaviour in my lesson. I intend taking extra time to sort things out."

Use eye contact:
> In normal conversations we rarely look at each other for more than one or two seconds, and the listener looks more than the speaker. In confrontations the aggressor may stare

aggressively to heighten the emotional tension. They may even demand it, "Look at me." Beware of this. Adolescents will know that they can take the high ground and fuel your frustration by refusing to look at you. Stay with the issue. If appropriate make notes and maintain frequent, but brief, eye contact with the child.

Through using these behaviours you are building a more positive relationship, or in the jargon, "non-verbal rapport building".

The more we can control our behaviour the more we will have a positive influence on the child's . The above ideas are not theoretical: they are obtained through minutely observing teachers who manage confrontations effectively and go home each night feeling calm and confident. Practise any you feel might be useful.

What to think and what to say
If a child is beginning to become confrontational then it is appropriate to try to talk with them, to ask,

"What is upsetting you?"

"Let's have a quiet five minutes together and see if we can sort things out."

At this stage we are showing both our concern and our desire to sort out their difficulty. This is when we can use listening skills. These skills involve us in checking things out, we are not just listening but showing the child that we are keen to understand what it is that they are telling us.

"I'm not sure I understand, could you tell me a little more?"

"Let me see if I've got the gist of what you're telling me. You are upset because…"

If a child is angry it can be helpful to reflect both our understanding and sympathy. It is not always helpful to use "angry" to describe what they are feeling, "upset" may be better. It conveys sympathy which is a good way of building a caring relationship.

"I can see that you are very upset about being left out."

Reframing

Because of the scripts that we each carry we may see anger and confrontation as bad and negative. But anger is a natural emotion. It is part of the grieving process, a natural reaction to many losses we experience. We can be angry at social injustices and we can channel this anger into challenging these and creating a more just society. In the classroom there can be many reasons why a child is angry. Perhaps the work is too difficult. Perhaps they are so used to being in control that they are apprehensive about being told what to do. They may not be used to adults setting clear boundaries and expecting children to follow them. Are they testing you? Because aggressive confrontational behaviour can be a symptom of so many things, we should try to look behind the behaviour. Common causes of aggressive behaviour include:

- learning difficulties
- aggressive role models
- bullying
- depression
- abuse, emotional and/or sexual

Being angry is not the problem. Children just like adults have a right to feel angry. It is when that behaviour infringes the rights of other people that it becomes a problem. As a rule of thumb always use your emotional energy to be positive about them and your problem solving energy to tackle the issue. It is the behaviour which is the problem, not them. We need to let them know that we will work with them to enable them to improve their behaviour.

Wrong footing tactics

"All the best laid plans of mice and men…" Managing challenging confrontations is an art not a science. If it were a science we would all carry the manual with us. We know that there are strategies that will work with a pupil one day, but not the next. They can be a different child from yesterday and we can be different people as well. It is good therefore to have a few surprise tactics up your sleeve. The following are some that work because they are out of the ordinary. They wrong foot the child who is perhaps playing out their own "script".

Humour

The unexpected funny remark can break the tension and release all the pent-up frustration through laughter. But it can never be guaranteed to work.

For example:

"I'm sorry I'd love to stay and argue but I've got this staff meeting, could we do it same time tomorrow?"

"I knew when I got out of bed this morning that this was just not going to be my day."

"I can see that you're really angry but can we just finish this job and then you can have a really good shout, scream and stamp around?"

"If we're going to argue you're going to have to help me, because I really am not sure I'm going to be much good."

Novel questions
A question which is loosely linked to what is going on can break the mood and move things on.

"Before I forget does your mum/dad still support the same team?"

"Have you ever wondered how they got good arguments on Grange Hill?"

"I would like to practise my French while we argue, is that OK? Do you know many French words?"

This tactic also means that the adult asks the question and this is an important tactic in maintaining control of difficult situations.

Distractions - real or imagined
"Did you just see something big and blue flash past the window? Hold on while I go and look."

"Did you hear a noise then? It sounded like something or someone falling, quick let's go and see if anyone needs our help."

Surprise tactics
"I've suddenly remembered I had to return these books to the office, do me a big favour and just pop them back."

"Oh no, one of my contact lenses has just fallen out. Don't move, help me look, they're really expensive."

Each of these tactics aims to wrong foot the situation as much as the child. Conflict situations can almost run away with themselves. These tactics can cause everyone to stop for a legitimate reason. It gives the adult the chance to restart from a different point.

And finally

The *aide-mémoir* that follows contains many of the key points we have covered as well as some highly effective strategies that are known to work. As you continue to use your existing strategies as well as adding a few new ones you should always remember that while your efforts may not always work, they are the right things to do. Through using these methods and understanding some of the principles of confrontation you are reflecting a professional and caring attitude to an aspect of school life that is one of the toughest challenges we face.

(Remember these skills are transferable and will be equally useful with adults as well as children.)

Confrontation Inhibitors

These core skills will work to block aggressive and confrontational behaviour.

Non-verbal Behaviours
Check that your behaviour is saying what you want it to.

Listening Skills
When you actively listen you stay controlled while showing real concern as well as helping the child to take control of the situation.

Be Solution-Focused
Do you make it clear that you want to find a solution to the difficulty?

Token Concession
If appropriate make an admission that you "can see that they have a point", "well, I have to admit it could have been dealt with better." (Known in the jargon as the "1% technical error strategy".)

Friendly Gesture
Make a deliberate friendly gesture. "I'm going to lend you a special book of my mine which may help." "Tomorrow I will give up my break to help

you sort this out." It is hard to be angry with someone who is offering to do you a favour. (This is drawing on the "norm of reciprocity".)

Ask for their Help
Remember as the adult you will be seen as the expert by the child. Ask them for their ideas, "I've never dealt with this before, what would you do if you were me?" "If I came to you with this problem, what would you advise me to do?"

Focus on the Issue
Make it clear that you need their help to resolve the issue. Keep asking them to think about the issue, their behaviour, make a point of telling them that "they are OK", it's their behaviour that is the focus.

Compromise
Be prepared to show that you are looking for a way forward that is acceptable to all concerned, one where everyone feels a "winner".

Save Face
The older the child the more important it is to make sure that there is always a way out - anyone who feels cornered will become more aggressive.

References

Faupel, A. (1998) *Anger Management,* David Fulton Publishers: London.

Fogell, J. & Long, R. (1997) *Spotlight on Special Educational Needs: Emotional and Behavioural Difficulties,* NASEN: Tamworth.

Freed, A. (1976) *T.A. for Teens,* Jalmar Press: California.

Goldstein, A., Harootunian, B. & Conoley, J. (1994) *Student Aggression,* Guilford Press: London.

Long, R. & Fogell, J. (1999) *Supporting Pupils with Emotional Difficulties,* David Fulton Publishers: London.